D1744387

# The Cambrian Coast
# Pwllheli–Harlech

Editor: Ioan Roberts

Gwasg Carreg Gwalch

First published in 2017
© text: Ioan Roberts
© publication: Gwasg Carreg Gwalch 2017

ISBN: 978-1-84524-244-2
Cover design: Eleri Owen
Map: Alison Davies
Published by Gwasg Carreg Gwalch,
12 Iard yr Orsaf, Llanrwst, Wales LL26 0EH
tel: 01492 642031
email: llanrwst@carreg-gwalch.com
website: www.carreg-gwalch.com

**Achnowledgements**

The publishers wish to acknowledge their gratitude
for these images:
Marian Delyth, p. 2
Tony Jones, p. 53, 77, 81, 127
Oriel Rob Piercy, 97
Visit Wales (© Crown copyright (2016)), p1, 18, 20,
27, 37, 38, 39, 47, 64, 67, 68, 69, 80, 87, 88, 89, 99,
103, 110, 113, 114, 115, 119, 121.

*Borth-y-gest*

# Contents

Pwllheli–Harlech   6
End of the line   8
'Salt Lake City'   10
Ships ahoy   12
Saints and Campers   16
The cottage boy   20
'I played football with Lloyd George'   23
Cromlech and ice-cream   26
Land of our fathers   28
The Age of Saints   32
Princes   34
Cricieth Castle   36
Return of the Welsh   40
Ospreys   42
Sea and mountain   46
Legends of stones and lakes   48
Tomen y Mur and Sarn Elen   50
Maen Twrog and the Celtic Saints   52
Turning back the tide from Traeth Mawr   56

Building a quay in the sand   60
Slates from Cambrian rocks   62
The Ffestiniog Railway   66
Shipbuilding   70
The shadow of the Western Front   74
The Tranquil Lakes   78
Chwarel Llechwedd today   82
Highland Railway and the Maritme Museum   86
Y Plas and the National Park   92
Craftsmen today and yesterday   96
Portmeirion   98
Storms and blue sky   102
Ancient stones   104
The church in the sands   108
A Norman Castle   112
The home and senedd of Owain Glyndŵr   118
The Manorhouses of Ardudwy   122
The Drovers' Roads   126

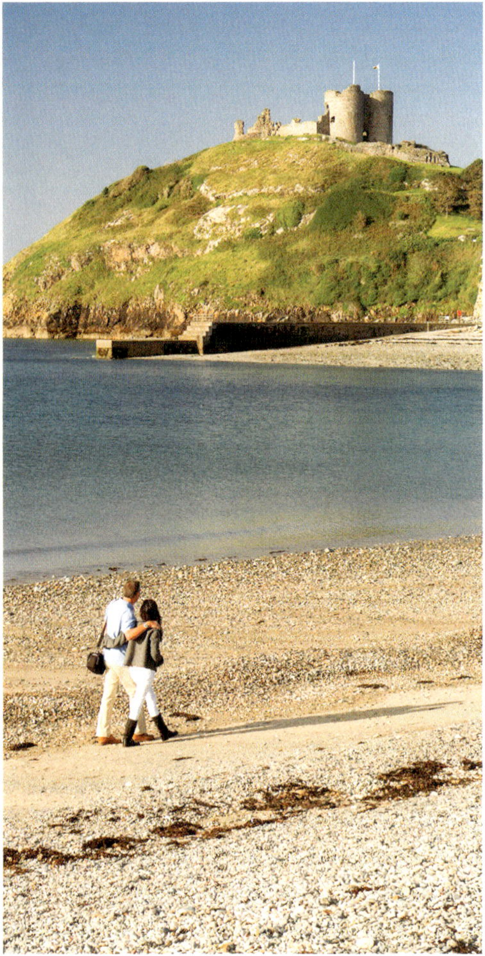

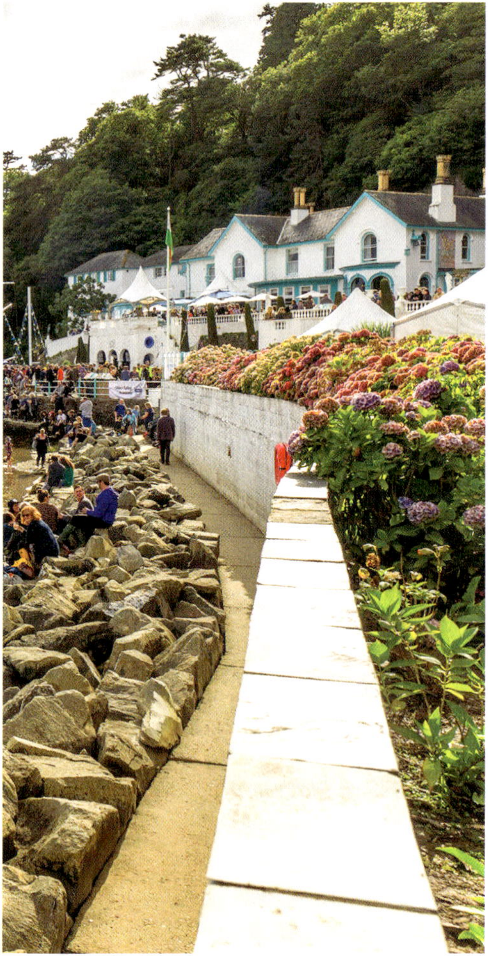

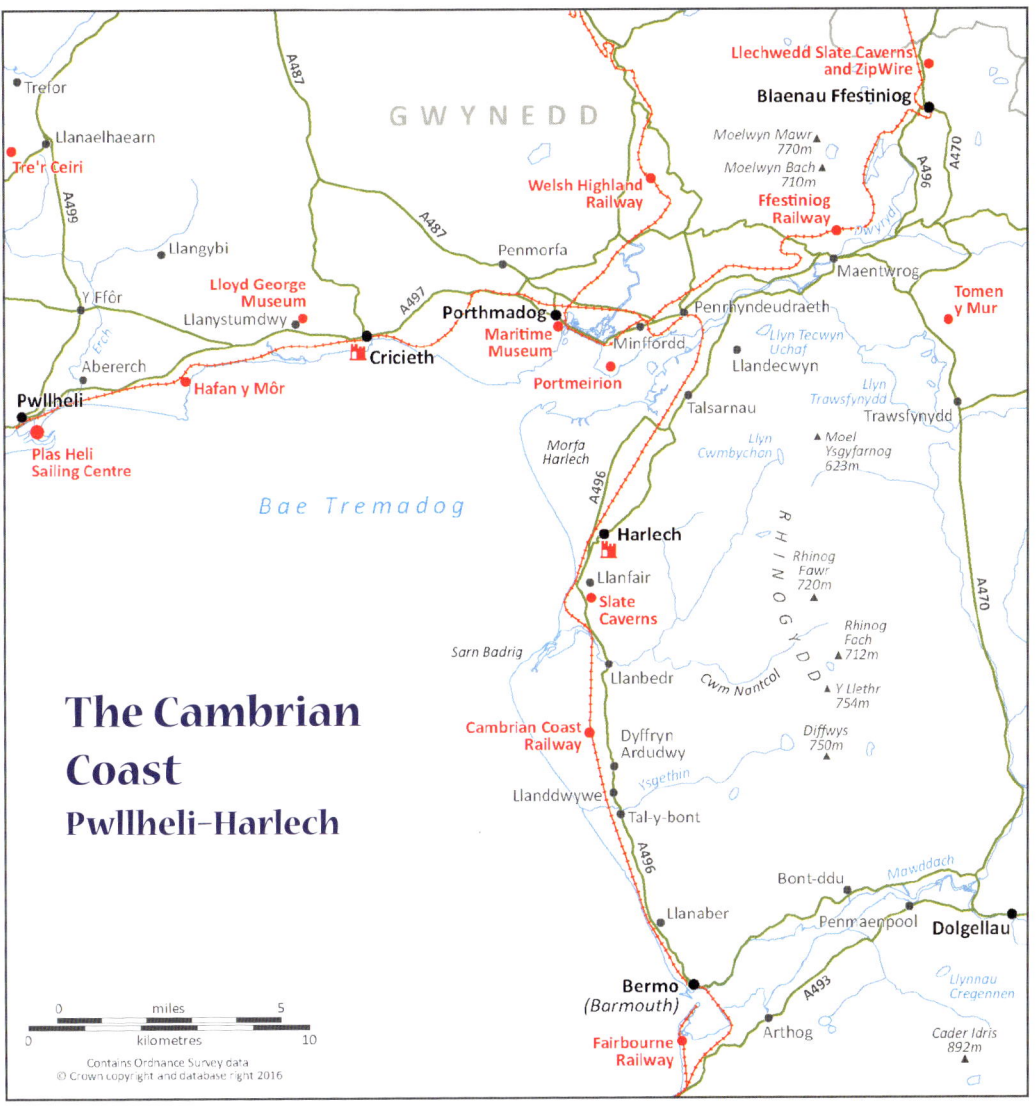

# Pwllheli-Harlech

'*Cambria*' was what the Romans called *Cymru* (Wales), and 'Cambrian Coast' has no clearly defined limits. Does it include the whole coastline of the country, from Prestatyn to the Severn Bridge? Is it just the western seaboard, linking the peninsulas of Llŷn in the north and Pembrokeshire in the south? To most people it is neither of these, but is identified with the Cambrian Coast Railway and its two branches connecting Pwllheli and Aberystwyth. During its 150-year history this line has survived the Beeching axe and other bureaucratic threats, and continues to provide one of the most picturesque train journeys you will find anywhere.

This book is not just about the railway, but covers an area loosely based on the northern section of the line, from Pwllheli to Harlech. With the sea on one side and the hills and mountains of Snowdonia National Park on the other, the train winds its way through a remarkable variety of landscapes and communities. We sometimes take a detour from the railway to the slate quarries and harsher climate further inland.

Whether you explore the area by rail, by car, on your bike or on foot, the book will guide you through some of the place-names, history and culture of the area, and introduce some of the some of the people and events that left their marks on the landscape.

Another volumes in the series continue the journey south to Aberystwyth.

*Early rail posters along the Cambrian Coast railway*

# HARLECH CASTLE

MERIONETH

Open to the public all the year round. Weekdays at 9.30 a.m.
Sundays 2 p.m. Admission: Adults 1'-, Children under 14 years 6d.

**TRAIN TO HARLECH STATION**
which is in close proximity to the Castle

# End of the line

The Arriva train to Pwllheli provides a regular tongue-twisting challenge to platform announcers in Birmingham or Wolverhampton, charged with naming every station along the way. Some who make the announcements on the train itself also struggle with Llwyngwril, Morfa Mawddach, Talsarnau, Llandecwyn, Penrhyndeudraeth, Minffordd and Penychain. This has been a longstanding bone of contention with language campaigners, and a few basic lessons in pronouncing Cymraeg would benefit everyone.

Pwllheli station, the first or last on the line depending where you live, had its official opening on Monday, July 12 1909, an occasion described by the Mayor as 'the most glorious day in the history of the town'. Huge crowds filled the streets and the newly built station square known as Pen Cob as the first train, decorated with flowers, carried VIPs from Afon-wen, all of two miles up the track. Schools and businesses closed for the day, the Porthmadog Brass Band led a procession through the town, Lloyd George and Winston Churchill sent goodwill telegrams. A local newspaper she day as vindication of Thomas Pennant's opinion, in an 1810 book, that Pwllheli was 'the best town in this country'. Three weeks after the opening nearly 4,000 trippers arrived in Pwllheli by train in one day and the station master and his staff were widely praised for the way they dealt with the stampede.

The euphoria was all the more remarkable bearing in mind that Pwllheli had already had a train service for over 40 years. The first locomotive, the Castell Deudraeth, was carried to the town on a ship in 1865. On a short length of newly-aid rails it pulled a row of trucks packed with people to nearby Abererch. Two years later Pwllheli's first station was opened, half a mile from the town centre near what is now the Glan-don Industrial Estate. A signal box from the early days is still standing and older residents refer to the location as 'yr hen stesion' (the old station).

That station had also generated huge excitement in its day, but never lived up to expectations. To get from the train to the town centre involved a trek through soggy ground liable to flood at high tide. The 1908 extension of the line overcame that

and was part of a development that included an embankment, floodgates and a new harbour.

Pwllheli was not intended to be the final terminal. Plans had been prepared as far back as the 1840s for a railway line beyond the town and across the Llŷn peninsula to Porth Dinllaen, which had been rejected in favour of Holyhead as the main port linking London and Dublin. As a result of the decision Porth Dinllaen was declining rapidly as a port and Pwllheli remains the end of the line.

*Pwllheli station*

*Porth Dinllaen harbour*

# 'Salt Lake City'

Shoppers who park their cars and their trolleys in front of the Asda supermarket in Pwllheli may not realise it, but this is the spot that gave the town its name. Back in the 13th Century much of the present town was submerged in sea water, including this sheltered area which became known as Llawr y Gors (*floor of the swamp*) or Pwll Heli (*brine pool*), the latter becoming the name of the settlement that began to develop into a town. In Victorian times when English names became fashionable among a section of the population, organisers of a local Eisteddfod set a competition to find the best English name for Pwllheli. One competitor, tongue in cheek, suggested Salt Lake City. The idea was abandoned.

Some of Pwllheli's street names date from the days before the construction of embankments and floodgates enabled land to be reclaimed from the sea. Y Traeth (*the beach*) and Lôn Dywod (*sandy lane*) are now some distance from the shore. A street known informally as Stryd Llygod (*street of mice*) lies behind The Mitre pub in the centre of town. The is a throwback from the days when ships used to anchor in that part of town, and the cargo of grain and other delicacies attracted vermin.

The first recorded reference to Pwllheli dates from the period that followed the killing in 1282 of Llywelyn ap Gruffudd, the last Prince of Wales at Cilmeri, Powys. The victorious Edward I commissioned an inventory of his newly acquired properties, which showed that the 21 families who lived in Pwllheli owned, between them, two fishing boats and 27 fishing nets.

Pwllheli had a long history as an administrative centre before the conquest. In mediaeval times the Welsh princes built motte and bailey castles throughout Wales. The name Penmownt, where a chapel stands today, possibly indicates the site of one of these castles. 'Llys' is the word for 'court', and the names Gadlys, a row of houses adjoining Penlan car park, and Henllys, a farm overlooking the town, confirm the belief that the tywysogion had courts in the area.

In 1355 Edward the Black Prince gave Pwllheli its charter as a borough. This brought certain privileges to the residents and granted permission to hold two annual fairs and a weekly Sunday market.

Fairs had actually been held in the town long before this. An open air market is still held on Wednesdays throughout the year, and also on Sundays in the summer.

*Hafan Pwllheli – boat anchorages in the old post of Pwllheli today*

# Ships ahoy

In the 18th and 19th centuries, Pwllheli developed into one of the main shipbuilding centres in Wales with more than 400 ships built here between 1759 and 1878. The industry reached its peak in 1840, with 28 ships built and 14 launched during the year. One of the few remaining signs of the boom is the imposing tower on the now closed Baptist chapel, built by William Jones the druggist, one on the main shipbuilders.

The launch of a ship was always a major event, and schools closed for the day. it was often accompanied by drunken revelry. This did not go down well with William Jones with his strong Baptist convictions. The night before one of his ships, the William Carey, was launched in 1848, he insisted that its crew of 25 attended a seiat or prayer meeting in Capel Penmownt to seek blessing for the new vessel. But other men in the town felt aggrieved because they had been refused a job on the ship. They adjourned to a pub for an alternative meeting, a notorious occasion remembered in the town's folklore as *Noson y Seiat Feddw* ('the night of the drunken seiat').

The increasing marine activity inevitably left its mark on the life of the town. It soon had far more public houses than required to serve the local community. According to the leading expert on Pwllheli's history, D. G. Lloyd Hughes (See *Pwllheli: An old Welsh town and it history*), there were 12 named pubs in the town in 1666 when the population was less than 300. Of the 10 pubs listed in 1784, the only existing one is Penlan Fawr, the town's oldest building. The interior has been transformed in recent years but its frontage is largely unchanged. The Whitehall, built in 1818, has also retained its exterior character although the interior has been tastefully renovated as a pub and restaurant.

The flourishing drinks trade brought a reaction in the shape of the Temperance Movement, whose influence forced some of the pubs to close their doors. One of the movement's leaders was Henry Jones Williams of Y Ffôr, better known by his bardic name, Plenydd. In his autobiography he describes addressing a temperance meeting in Pwllheli, when a drunken farmer from Llŷn joined the audience. The visitor objected to the speaker's suggestion that the town's hotels should stop selling strong drink. 'Where am I going to keep my horse next time I'm in town?' enquired the farmer. 'Next time you come to town,' replied Plenydd, 'take your horse to the bar of the Crown, and take yourself to the stable.'

It was technology that brought about the demise of the shipbuilding industry. Steam displaced sail, steel ships replaced wooden ones, and the train provided a new means of carrying slates to larger ports in England for shipment worldwide. The last two ships built at Pwllheli were completed in 1878.

Pwllheli's sailors had shown enormous skills and courage all over the world. But there were hazards in home waters as well, notably Sarn Badrig (*St Patrick's Causeway*). Sometimes visible at low tide, this reef extends across Cardigan Bay from Mochras in Meirionnydd towards Ynys Enlli (*Bardsey*). Sarn Badrig is a sailor's nightmare and was the final resting place of many ships. At the end of the nineteenth century a famous lifeboat designer called Henry Richardson came to

*Sarn Badrig*

live in a house called Bryn Hyfryd, the old home of William Jones the Druggist. When Richardson died, one of his lifeboats, an open rowing boat, was presented to the town, and a shed erected to store it. This was the start of the lifeboat service, still an important part of the town's life.

Pwllheli once had a busy fishing industry with its community of colourful characters. To survive they had to develop a detailed knowledge of the bay and the natur of the sea bed: where to cast their nets without getting into trouble and where to ctch different tupes of fish. With no electronic devices they had to navigate using natural landmarks luch as mountain peaks and the tower of the Baptist chapel.

Towards the end of the 19th century fishermen from the north west of England began to visit Pwllheli regularly, some of them marrying local women and settling in the area. There was probably an element of overfishing leading to a decline in stocks and in the number of local fishermen. Today there are few full-time fishermen in the town. But many people still set their lobster pots, and local restaurants and hotels are putting more emphasis on local produce.

The area has adapted well to changing habits, and sailing for pleasure is now a major contributor to the local economy. Young people learn marine skills at the sixth form college, Coleg Meirion Dwyfor, grasping the opportunities offered by one of the best sailing venues in the UK. The town had a major boost in 2015 with the opening of Plas Heli, the Welsh National Sailing Academy, which hosts national and international events.

You will find more details of the history of Pwllheli and things to do in the district in another book in this series, *Exploring Pwllheli and Llŷn*.

*1. Plas Heli, the new sailing centre; 2. An International sailing competition at Pwllheli; 3. Penlan, the oldest inn in Pwllheli.*

# Saints and Campers

Afon Erch, which marks the boundary between Llŷn and the commote of Eifionydd, divides the pretty village of Abererch in half. ('Aber' – the mouth of a river). The village church dates from the 6th century and was established by the Celtic saint, Cawrdaf. It is one of several churches in north-west Wales where pilgrims used to rest on their way to the holy island of Bardsey.

Abererch also has an intriguing link with *Yr Hen Ogledd* ('Old North'), an area of northern England and southern Scotland inhabited by Brythonic tribes in the post Roman period. These people spoke a Brythonic language, the ancestor of Welsh, and produced what is regarded as the earliest surviving Welsh poetry. Rhydderch Hael (*hael*: generous) was a famous king of *Yr Hen Ogledd* and Abererch is one of the places where he is reputed to have been buried. Similar claims have been made about the cromlech (*dolmen*) in nearby Y Ffôr and Stranraer in Scotland. One argument in favour of Abererch is provided by the unlikely source of Manx fishermen who used to visit the Pwllheli area in the second half of the 19th century. These were devout Christians who never went fishing on Sundays. During their stay they would always visit the church at Abererch to pay homage to Rhydderch, who was a hero in the Isle of Man after he helped defeat a Northumbrian king in a battle at the end of the 6th century. Thirteen centuries later he was still rememberd by the fishermen, who were convinced that he was laid to rest under a stone north of the altar in St Cawrdaf's church.

During the Second World War the Ministry of Defence asked the entrepreneur Billy Butlin to build a training base for the Navy at Penychain, near Chwilog. The camp – on dry land – was named *HMS Glendower* and after the war the site was returned to Butlin to expand his holiday camp empire. In its heyday in the 1950s and 60s the campers far outnumbered the permanent residents of Pwllheli, but they remained largely behind a high fence in their self-contained

*1. St Cawrdaf's Church, Abererch;*
*2. Cromlech at Y Ffôr; 3. Cawrdaf – the Saint's well.*

enclave with its own entertainment. It was only on Wednesdays, market day, that the campers flocked to Pwllheli and the Crosville bus company made a fortune ferrying them back and forth.

On Saturdays, when the chalets were vacated and prepared for new arrivals, local children would earn pocket money carrying campers' luggage between the camp and their buses and trains. On those days the tiny Penychain station was possibly the busiest on the Cambrian Coast. It was also one of the most mispronounced, with many of its users unwittingly grating on the ears of Welsh speakers by calling it 'Penny Chain'.

After the camp closed at the end of the season the gates would be thrown open to admit local people for the annual Eisteddfod Butlin, and bars like the Pig and Whistle became Welsh for one day.

Towards the end of the 20th century holiday habits had changed and Butlin's is rebranded as the Hafan y Môr Caravan Holiday Park. But for former campers, Redcoats, chalet maids and Glamorous Granny and Knobbly Knees contestants, the place will forever be Butlin's.

'*Pen ychain*' means 'ox's head 'and the name probably derives from the shape of the headland. A more interesting theory is linked to Cantre'r Gwaelod, one of the best known Welsh legends. Cantre'r Gwaelod, an enchanted land below sea level off this western coast, was drowned when a drunken night watchman called Seithenyn forgot to close the floodgates. An ancient poem describes the anguish of Gwyddno Garanhir, lord of Cantre'r Gwaelod, as his kingdom vanished beneath the waves. And the real name of the headland was not Pen-ychain but Pen-ochain – *headland of sighs*.

*Abererch sands*

# The cottage boy

If you inspect the top of the parapet wall of the bridge in Llanystumdwy very carefully, you may be able to find the letters D.Ll.G. M.P. carved roughly in the stone. The initials D.Ll.G. were sculpted when the village's most famous son was very young – possibly by David Lloyd George himself. When the 27 year-old Liberal candidate won a famous by-election victory in Caernarfon Boroughs in 1890, defeating the local Tory landowner by 18 votes, the village blacksmith got carried away. He rushed out of his smithy brandishing a hammer and chisel and added the letters M.P. to the inscription.

Born in Manchester in 1863, David Lloyd George moved to Llanystumdwy with his mother and sister the following year after his schoolmaster father died. They lived with his mother's brother Richard Lloyd, the village cobbler, in a cottage called Highgate. The career path from the cottage to 10 Downing Street was the stuff of legend, although historian Emyr Price warns against exaggerating the family's poverty. Uncle Lloyd the shoemaker had two men working for him, and although poor compared to the landowning classes in the neighbourhood, they were better off than farm labourers' families who were in the majority.

The young Dafydd had shown signs of political radicalism very early on. At the age of five he carried a Liberal banner in Llanystumdwy to celebrate another election victory. Later he led a rebellion in the Church School in Llanystumdwy against reciting the Catechism, which was anathema to nonconformist children. The rector and local squire witnessed this act of defiance, the squire being none other than Sir Hugh John Ellis-Nanney of Plas Gwynfryn, the Conservative who was defeated by Lloyd George in 1890.

Plas Gwynfryn, the most imposing mansion in the area in its day, is now derelict, whereas Highgate cottage is thriving as part of the Lloyd George Museum. There are items tracing the career of Lloyd George form a fiery country solicitor representing the underprivileged to his rapid rise in

*1. David Lloyd George's Museum, Llanystumdwy; 2. The Prime Minister's childhood home; 3. Lloyd George's grave.*

*Tŷ Newydd writing centre*

Wizard who could do no wrong was badly tarnished later in life. Some compatriots accused him of betraying his youthful Welsh patriotism, his stock plummeted in Ireland for his handling of the Treaty negotiations that partitioned the country, he was exposed for selling knighthoods and peerages to fund the Liberal party, and his now well-publicised womanising would probably never have survived the battering of today's tabloid newspapers.

But his heroic status among many of his countrymen as the cottage boy who never lost his burning ambition to improve the lives of the needy remains intact. There are some who still remember the words of an election song from one of his campaigns:

> *Pwy rodd bensiwn I hen bobol?*
> *Lloyd George, David Lloyd George,*
> *Fotiwn i gyd i David Lloyd George.*

[Who gave a pension to old people? Lloyd George, David Lloyd George, we're all going to vote for David Lloyd George].

A few years before his death, aged 83, in August 1945, Lloyd George and his second wife Frances had moved to live in Tŷ

Parliament. As Chancellor of the Exchequer in 1909 he introduced his 'People's Budget' bringing in the old age pension and laying the foundation of the Welfare State. As Minister of Munitions and later Prime Minister he played a key role in winning the First War.

It's been said that all political careers end in failure. Although not strictly true in the case of Lloyd George, his early reputation as the Dewin Dwyfor or Welsh

Newydd, Llanystumdwy, now home to the National Writing Centre for Wales. It was from there that his coffin was carried on a farm cart to a spot he had selected himself on the bank of Afon Dwyfor where he used to play as a child. Officially a state funeral, it was not what is normally associated with such occasions. There were thousands of mourners, some of them having climbed trees to get a better view. Some of his grandchildren who were serving in the Second World War were in their uniforms, but news footage does not indicate a strong military presence. At the graveside the crowd sang Cwm Rhondda in the mother tongue of the former Prime Minister, the only Welsh speaker ever to have held that position.

# 'I played football with Lloyd George'

Less well-known universally than Lloyd George, but also a legend among his own people, the writer and playwright William Samuel Jones was born in Llanystumdwy in 1920 and never lived more than a mile from the village. He left school at 14 to train as a mechanic. But he had a natural genius for words, and went on to produce some of the best Welsh-language literature of his era.

He started writing humorous sketches for local youth groups in the early 1950s and won prizes for satirical poems at the National Eisteddfod. His talent was spotted by the writer and BBC producer Emyr Humphreys. who commissioned him to write radio plays for the Welsh Home Service. In the 1960s Wil, his artist brother Elis Gwyn Jones, Emyr Humphreys and other friends established a little theatre called Y Gegin ('The Kitchen') in Cricieth, inspired by similar ventures that Wil had seen during visits to Dublin. He wrote plays specifically for Y Gegin audiences and was often compared with Irish writers like Sean O'Casey and Brendan Behan.

His small garage in Llanystumdwy became a popular meeting place for local characters whose mannerisms and sayings became a priceless source of material for his writing. He befriended visiting tramps, and even unwelcome callers such as taxmen and planning officers unwittingly contributed to his plays and short stories.

At the age of 40 he sole the garage and moved to a bungalow at nearby Rhos-lan with his wife and two young daughters, becoming the first person in the modern era to earn a living by writing exclusively in Welsh. He found the going tough at first, remarking that handling a biro was harder than handling a spanner. He spent what leisure time he had in a shed repairing and renovating old bikes and motor bikes. He also took delight in taking groups of friends on a guided cycling trip through Eifionydd, entertaining them with reminiscences and anecdotes at every corner.

His best-known literary creation was Ifas y Tryc, a self-important small businessman played by his friend, Cricieth actor Stewart Jones. They collaborated on hundreds of scripts, and Stewart used to say that Wil had never handed him a bad one. Ifas became a cult figure on radio and television, on stage and in books.

The establishing of Welsh-language TV Channel S4C in 1982 created new opportunities for writers and enabled Wil to write many acclaimed plays. Although comedy was his main forte, many of his creations had deeper meanings and showed a sharp observation of human nature. He published an autobiography and several books, three of which were launched simultaneously in the village hall at Llanystumdwy when their author was aged 85.

To many within his community he is remembered not so much for his writing as for his wit, humanity and enthralling company, especially in Llanystumdwy pub Tafarn y Plu (*Feathers Inn*).

The pub is almost opposite the Lloyd George Museum, prompting some visitors to ask Wil if he had ever met his famous compatriot. 'Oh yes,' Wil would reply, 'I played football with him!'

He was telling the truth. Lloyd George had paid a visit to his old school in Llanystumdwy when Wil was a pupil there. The boys were kicking a ball in the yard and Lloyd George joined in, with Wil claiming to have shoulder-charged the famous man.

*Wil Sam, the renowned writer*

# Cromlech and ice-cream

From a lay-by at the top of Allt Caerdyni, the hill that leads down into Cricieth from the Porthmadog side, you can see every period in the town's history in an instant. Below you on the left, squatting like a hare in the gorse, there is a tiny cromlech from the very ancient past. In the shadow of the castle lies Cadwaladr's Ice Cream shop. Between the two there are rough-hewn fishermen's cottages and the splendid homes of Victorian ship captains and merchants. Up the sun-drenched hillside to the right are the white villas of the well-to-do 20th century Welsh.

Cricieth did not fare too well as an English colony in the Middle Ages after the fall of Llywelyn. In 1403, as we shall see, the castle was burned by Owain Glyndŵr, and it's been a ruin ever since.

In fact, prosperity only came with the arrival of the railway in 1868. For a century after that Cricieth, the Pearl of Wales, enjoyed a boom with its castle, beach and famous ice-cream. And the golden age hasn't completely disappeared.

*1. The double towers of the castle entrance;*
*2. Cricieth Castle.*

# Land of our fathers

Very little is known of the people who lived in this corner of the world before the Celts arrived. It's likely that a tribe settled on the peaks of Yr Eifl, a bit further west, between 8,000 a 4,000 BC, who were related to the Basques with their origins in the Stone Age. The same civilization has left its mark in meini hirion [standing stones], cromlechi and arrow heads all over Europe.

The maen hir at Pentre Felin is 9 feet long, allegedly the longest in Wales. It wasn't always located here. The date 1721 is carved on it and local legend has it that the sons of Cefnmeysydd Isa' farm had erected it there in memory of their mother. There is also a notable stone at Betws Fawr farm, and yet another at Parc Ladi, Glasfryn, and the latter associated with a very sad legend as we shall see.

Cromlechi are what remains of the graves of chieftains of early tribes. Originally these were covered by large mounds of earth. The one at Cefn Isa, Rhoslan dates from around 3000 BC. The cromlech at Ystumcegid known locally as Coetan Arthur is not quite so old but a lot more majestic! in the old days there was a long passage leading up to it. That small cromlech at Caerdyni has still not been 'classified' by the experts. And at the base of Mynydd Ednyfed, near the golf course, there is a stone circle shaped like a ship that is not recorded on any map.

The earliest evidence of the Celts, as in other areas, is hillforts. There was nearly one on every tiny hilltop! The largest is Garn Bentyrch in Llangybi, where the sturdy walls can still be seen. In Cricieth there was a fortress on top of Caerdyni hill and another on a large rock known to this day as Dinas, which means… 'fortress'. But who were the enemies?

Experts today tend to accept the old tradition that Cunedda came from *Yr Hen Ogledd* in the 4th century, as part of a strategic plan at the end of the Roman occupation and to expel the Irish from Wales. And yet the Irish and Brythoniaid must have lived side by side here for centuries, as they did in parts of Dyfed. At Llystyn Gwyn, Bryncir, there is a bilingual stone commemorating a certain Icorix. If the sun shines in the right direction you

*1. Ystumcegid Cromlech; 2. Caerdyni Cromlech; 3. Rhoslan Cromlech.*

can see that inscription from the 6th century in Latin and also in the ancient Irish Ogham alphabet. And it's possible that a muddled folk memory is reflected in the name *Cytiau'r Gwyddelod* ('huts of the Irish') for the round houses whose remnants are still visible on some of the hillforts. There is also a 6th century Latin inscribed stone at Gesail Gyfarch.

*1. Garn Bentyrch, Llangybi; 2. Llystyn Gwyn Stone; 3. 6th century latin stone at Gesail Gyfarch.*

# The Age of Saints

The name of the area in northern Eifionydd which includes Penmorfa and Cefn Coch, where there were two large stone circles in ancient times, is Penyfed. 'Nyfed' in the age of *Derwyddon* (Druids) meant holy bush. It was to these places that Saints came to preach the Gospel.

The church in Penmorfa is dedicated to Beuno. But he moved on to Clynnog Fawr yn Arfon. Another saint, Cybi, turned left along a path that had been well trodden by pilgrims on their way to Bardsey. Ffynnon Ddunod is on this road, and a farm called Bach y Saint was said to provide lodgings for the pilgrims.

It was near the well of the Celtic fort at Garn Bentyrch that Cybi built his cell, establishing the community which in due course became Llangybi. The old saint is in good fettle judging by the Council's bilingual sign: Ffynnon Gybi/'Cybi's Well'!

Some distance up the steep path through the oak trees towards the fort there is a big rock where the saint used to meditate. But he did not die in this magical place. He moved to Anglesey to establish another cause among the ruins of a Roman fort that bears his name, Caergybi (*Holyhead*).

The nave of Llangybi church dates from the end of the 15th century, but the chancel is much older. By the porch a cross has been carved in a stone in the style of the 7th – 9th century. Some believe that the building, shaped like a giant beehive, also dates from the pre-Norman period. There has probably been a church on this spot ever since the first primitive building was erected in the age of the saints.

In the 18th century a small cottage was built nearby to provide a home for the well-keeper and accommodation for pilgrims. At that time the remedial qualities of the water attracted hundreds who were ill or depressed. Young women trying to read the minds of their lovers would drop a handkerchief on the surface of the water. If it floated due south, the lads were honest and faithful; due north and they were lying. Sometime early in the 19th century some rascal pulled a large eel from the wafer, and people said that the remedial powers of the water had been drained away.

Other saints came to Eifionydd.

Garmon travelled from Britanny to build his cell in what is now Llanarmon. The present church at Llanystumdwy was built in 1862, but there are records of a church on the site, dedicated to Sant Ioan (John) in the 14th century. 'Dwy' in the name of the village has the same meaning as 'dwyfol' – 'divine' – suggesting that this was the site of a Celtic church similar to earlier ones at Llangybi and Llanarmon.

*Ffynnon Gybi*

# Princes

The commote of Eifionydd has been described in a well-known poem by R Williams Parry as '*y fro rhwng môr a mynydd*' – the land between the sea and the mountain. It stretches from the vicinity of Porthmadog in the east to Afon Erch in the west, from the top of Cwm Pennant in the north down to the sea. Before Edward l dismantled the old Welsh administrative order in 1284 Eifionydd formed half of the *cantref* (medieval administrative division – hundred) of Dunoding. Ardudwy was the other half.

Eifionydd was also the territory of Collwyn ap Tangno in the 11th century. Collwyn was head of the 'fifteen tribes of Gwynedd' – and it was to him that everyone of note in Eifionydd sought to trace their ancestry. There is a farm called Cefn Collwyn not far from Cricieth.

Nant Cyll in Pant Glas was the site of a large and bloody battle mentioned in one of the tales of the Mabinogi, between two chieftains, Math and Pryderi. Pant Glas today is better known as the childhood home of singer Bryn Terfel.

The court of early chieftains was possibly in the fort known as Garn Bentyrch, but the administrative centre of Eifionydd was in Dolbenmaen, where the old Roman Road crosses Afon Dwyfor. A large mound of earth in the motte-and-baily style is still visible there. Prince Llywelyn Fawr (c. 1172 – 1240) probably had a court there, but in 1230, he moved his court and all his officials to a new castle he'd built on a rock in Cricieth.

The battle between Math a Phryderi was not the only skirmish before the end of Welsh independence. In 1255, Llywelyn ap Gruffudd clashed with his brothers Owain and Dafydd, and defeated them in battle at Drws Daufynydd in the Pant Glas area that was vividly described by a poet called Llygad Gŵr.

*1. Cwm Pennant;*
*2. Nant Cyll.*

HENDRE
NANTCYLL

# Cricieth Castle

The enormous gatehouse to Castell Cricieth, with sturdy towers on either side, gives some indication of the imposing fortress that once stood here. It used to be assumed that these magnificent structures were the work of Edward l. But the one in Cricieth was primarily the work of the Princes of Gwynedd, one of the few surviving castles built by the Welsh. It was the Cymry who wrecked it as well.

Edward's intention after the Conquest was to create an English borough in Cricieth, similar to the one in Conwy. It's believed that at one time he considered establishing the county headquarters in Cricieth rather than Caernarfon. In 1284, 'Crukyth' was granted a royal charter that allowed it to hold fairs and markets and required it to hold a court of law. Plots of land were offered to attract people there from England – but it was poor quality land. Ten years after the town was founded, Cricieth's population consisted of only nine men, 13 women and 19 children. It's unlikely that more than 100 people ever lived in the town during that period, and there was no need to enclose the town with a wall.

A clause in the charter insisted that the burgesses had to be English, a condition that proved difficult to enforce. In 1337 the Constable was ordered to expel three men from the town because they were Welsh, but in 1374 there were eight men with Welsh names sitting on the court jury. More remarkably, the Constable himself was a Welshman, albeit a staunchly royalist one: Sir Hywel ap Gruffudd, or Hywel y Fwyell ('the Axe'). He had been acclaimed for his bravery in the battle of Poitiers in 1356, capturing the King of France after chopping off his horse's head with his axe. He was rewarded with a royal allowance followed by rent from mills in Chester and the castle in 'Cryckiarth'. A famous poem to Hywel by Iolo Goch contrasts the lavish lifestyle in the castle in contrast with the harsh existence of the burgesses below.

Then in 1403, Owain Glyndŵr attacked Caernarfon Castle helped by ships from France. There, fighting on the English side, was a nobleman from Eifionydd, Ieuan ap

*The castle and the coastline*

Maredudd. He was killed defending the castle. But the walls at Caernarfon proved impregnable and Owain and his army decided to attack Cricieth instead, pausing on the way to burn two houses belonging to the hapless Ieuan. The foundations of Cefn y Fan are barely visible today in a corner of a field at Ymlwch Bach farm. But it's said that the remnants of a fire can still be seen on stones in Gesail Gyfarch. Anyone who sided with the King of England would have been ill advised to set foot in Eifionydd, and Ieuan's body had to be carried in a boat from Caernarfon to Traeth Mawr to be buried with his ancestors in Penmorfa.

*The Castle at Cricieth*

# Return of the Welsh

The upper part of Cricieth near the castle is kmown to this day as *Yr Hen Dref* (The old town). The patch of green by the entrance to the castle is *Gardd y Stocs* (Garden of Stocks) and opposite there is a house called *Porth yr Aur* (Golden gate) where the castle's Treasury once stood. At the top of the hill is the old town square where burgesses would hold a market to sell produce to the garrison. And on Lôn Bach, which leads down from the top end of the square there is a place called *Gardd yr Esgob* (Bishop's Garden) to remind us that Edward had given some land to the Bishop of Bangor. Then there are three cottages called *Tŷ Isaf* (Lower house), *Tŷ Canol* (Middle house) and... Sea Winds! These date in their present form from the 16th century but their foundations go back to the 14th century; they were builts on plots of land belonging to the original burgesses. Down towards the railway and the car park some of these plots are cultivated as gardens to this day. And across the Maes on the other side of the high street, fairs are still held twice a year, just as they were in the days of Hywel y Fwyell.

Eifionydd was staunchly loyal to Glyndŵr to the end, making it impossible for the Crown's finance officers to collect taxes here. For ten years after the town was decimated by the Welsh, Cricieth was an empty shell. There was no reason for anyone to stay here exposed to the wind tilling the land and tending their livestock when there was no longer a market for their produce. And there was no future for a colony in the heart of enemy territory without a royal garrison to defend it.

But seeing that Glyndŵr's war was finally over, a new generation began to settle in the town. The market, fair and court of law were resurrected. But the profit from the court now went to individuals who were Welsh, as were the new landowners. On the left half way up Allt y Castell is *Tŷ Mawr* (large house) which has been owned by the same family longer than any other house in Cricieth. The first record of anyone living here dates from the middle of the 15thd century, the exact period when Cricieth was being re-

*St Catherine's, Cricieth*

populated. The name of the owner then was Dafydd Llwyd. Although Cricieth had kept its charter and royal privileges, it was now completely Welsh, the same as the boroughs of Pwllheli and Nefyn, and descendants of the early burgesses have gone completely native.

Around this time too, proving that the parish was experiencing better times, St Catherine's church was considerably extended. This is some distance from the castle, and the likelihood is that there had been an early Celtic church on the site that had nothing to do with the castle. During Edward's period the church was consecrated to the Norman Saint, Catherine. Nearby at the top of the Maes, ther is an ancient well with steps leading down to the water. That was called Ffynnon y Saint (*the Saint's well*). But it is likely that it once bore the name of one particular saint. If that saint's name could be discovered the church could be returned to its rightful owner!

# Ospreys

Two unexpected visitors from Africa arrived on the banks of Afon Glaslyn near Llanfrothen in 2004, paving the way for a highly popular wildlife attraction. The arrivals were the first pair of breeding ospreys seen in Wales for almost a century. They have been making the perilous journey from West Africa to the same spot regularly ever since.

Ospreys had been extinct in Britain since 1916 but were reintroduced in Scotland in 1956. At the beginning of this century some of the birds were spotted in summer over the Glaslyn valley, and in May 2004 a pair was found nesting in an oak tree near Pont Croesor. This caused much excitment among bird lovers and the RSPB organised 24-hour surveillance to safeguard the site. To prevent disturbance of the pair, a fenced viewing area was constructed about a mile from the nest, with powerful telescopes provided. Then on June 30th a violent storm caused the nest to collapse killing the two chicks. The parents began to rebuild their nest but did not attempt to breed again that year. The public viewing area remained open and attracted 9500 visitors in the eight weeks it was open.

By the time the pair returned the following year RSPB staff and volunteers, including local schoolchildren, had built an artificial nest on a platform in the tree. A CCTV camera was attached to the nest so that the birds could be observed closely by visitors and staff. The pair returned in the spring and bred the first successful Welsh brood. Since then they have come back every March, the male usually arriving a couple of days before the female. By 2014 visitor numbers had reached over 75,000 a year and a total of 26 chicks had been raised.

In 2013 the RSPB withdrew from the Glaslyn project to re-prioritise their resources in order to protect other birds threatened with extinction. A group of wildlife enthusiasts agreed to take the reins and run the project at a local level. Bywyd Gwyllt Glaslyn Wildlife (BGGW) was set up as a community interest company to continue the work.

In 2014 work began on the

*Glaslyn Osprey project*

construction of a new visitor centre at Pont Croesor, which was opened the following year. The public viewing scheme is open between April and the end of August. There is no admission charge but donations are invited. Apart from one employee, the work is conducted entirely by volunteers and costs around £1,000 a week to run.

Two other osprey centres have now been established in Wales, one near Welshpool and the other at Cors Dyfi near Machynlleth, which is featured in another book in this series.

*Afon Glaslyn from Pont Croesor*

# Sea and mountain

From the marshes of Traeth Mawr and Traeth Bach to the summit of Moelwyn Mawr and Moelwyn Bach, there is a mystical air about the land between Porthmadog and Harlech. The rugged mountains of Eryri form an impressive backdrop on all sides and are sometimes reflected in the waters of the estuaries. Ancient heroes would come out of the mist, loiter awhile and then disappear; Celtic saints crossed the seas and built churches, and in a more recent industrial age, slates were hewn from the depths of the mountains and brought down to the sea to be exported to the four corners of the globe.

Crossing to another world is a common theme wherever the land and sea meet – the stories which connect the past to the present also transport us to another world. Once again in this ardal we see that an ancient culture and skills are to be found under the surface of what is visible to us today.

*Y Traeth Mawr and Glaslyn estuary*

# Legends of stones and lakes

The oldest stories of the Welsh – the Mabinogi – tell of a war between the province of Dyfed (south-western Wales) and Gwynedd after the magician, Gwydion, stole pigs belonging to Pryderi, king of Dyfed, by deception. The two armies met on either side of the estuary of Afon Dwyryd, and instead of instigating a mass slaughter, it was decided to resolve the argument by individual combat between Gwydion and Pryderi. Pryderi's physical strength was no match for Gwydion's magical powers – the king of Dyfed was slain and was buried above Felenrhyd near Maentwrog.

In the same story, we come across Lleu living with his wife Blodeuwedd, who was conjured out of flowers, in their court at Mur Castell. There are those who believe that the old Roman fort at Tomen y Mur between Llan Ffestiniog and Trawsfynydd stands on the site. Blodeuwedd is seduced by Gronw Pebr who was hunting deer in Cwm Cynfal and together they conspired to kill Lleu on the banks of Afon Cynwal. Lleu survived to take his revenge, and although Gronw tried to shield himself behind a rock, Lleu threw his spear with such force that it passed right through the rock, killing Gronw. Llech Gronw (*Gronw's slab*), a standing stone with a hole through it, can still be seen in Cwm Cynfal.

Two other local legends involve love and revenge. There was a dearth of women in Ardudwy when three young men went look for sweethearts. They left the coast and journeyed as far as Dyffryn Clwyd. There they found three very attractive young young girls. However, none of them seemed to fancy absconding with three wild lads from the west. So the youths abducted the women, forcing them to return with them to Ardudwy. During the journey however, the women's stance started to moderate slightly, and they began to talk of the harsh existence enforced upon them by their fathers and brothers. Before nightfall, their hearts had warmed and each of them had fallen in love with one of the youths from Ardudwy. That evening was spent on the banks of a lake above Ffestiniog. In the morning, the

*Llech Gronw, Cwm Cynfal*

women went to bathe in the lake and much to their distress they saw riders coming over the horizon. The riders galloped to their encampment and killed the men before their eyes. The women then recognised the riders as their fathers and their brothers, and as they tried to flee into the deeper waters of the lake out of the reach of their avenging relatives, all three drowned – hence the present-day Llyn y Morwynion (the maidens' lake).

There is a similar story in Llanfrothen.

Young men from Llŷn were killed there when they came in search of sweethearts, and the ground near the church is still known as Maes Gwŷr Llŷn (the field of the men of Llŷn).

# Tomen y Mur and Sarn Elen

The Celts established their trade routes and forts, and brought with them their talent for forging metals. Tomen y Mur near Trawsfynydd was a Celtic *caer* (fortress) before the Romans built their extensive camp on the site. They mined for copper in the rocks of Cwm Prysor, and a fine brass cup dating from the Celtic period has been found in Trawsfynydd. A copy can be seen at Canolfan Llys Ednowain, the community heritage centre.

One of the greatest contributions made by the Romans to Cymru was a road network over the hills connecting different regions with each other. Some of these must already have existed, but it was the Romans' methods of paving which made road travel so much easier. One of these was named after a Brythonic princess, Elen, who married a Roman official, and Sarn Elen was the name of the main road which connected northern Cymru with the south. Sarn Elen ran through central Meirionnydd from Dolwyddelan through Tomen y Mur towards Dolgellau. Another Roman road also ran through Tomen y Mur to Segontium (Caernarfon) in one direction and to Caer-gai (Llanuwchllyn) in the other.

The caer at Tomen y Mur stands at an important crossroad. The hillock on the present-day site appertains to a motte castle which was built there during the Norman period, and stands on the north-western wall of the Roman fort. It is an impressive site on a lofty escarpment, at the mercy of south-westerly winds, but dominating a wide area. The caer was originally built there in 78 AD, on four acres of ground. Later on, in 110 AD, it was reduced to three acres but stone walls were erected to protect it. The Romans left the fort in 140 AD.

To the north-east of the tomen (mound), at a bend in the road, are the remains of a Roman amphitheatre. Amphitheatre is perhaps rather a grandiose term as the circular base is only some 25 metres across, but this is the only example in Britain of a theatre in proximity to a small fort. In such a remote setting, theatrical entertainment would certainly have raised the spirits of the soldiers stationed there!

A hundred metres further down from the amphitheatre, there is a flat patch of ground. This was the exercise area for the garrison. The level of the ground was raised to create a broad platform for exercising. Further along Sarn Elen, there are traces of a bank that was built to support a bridge over Nant Tyddyn-yr-ynn. Beyond this earthwork are a number of small heaps about 30 cm in height; these are the remains of a Roman bath-house. What with exercise, entertainment and the bath-house, the troops at Tomen-y-Mur must have been kept fairly busy.

*Tomen y Mur*

# Maen Twrog and the Celtic Saints

Christianity reached Cymru during the era of Roman rule and the Celtic Church developed here during the Age of the Saints. The western seaboard was on an important highway during this period, and Celtic seintiau would journey back and forth between the early Christian communities in Wales, Brittany, Ireland, Cornwall and Scotland, undertaking pilgrimages as far as the Mediterranean.

These seintiau, to a much greater degree than the missionaries of the Church of Rome, were responsible for Wales becoming a Christian nation around the 4th to the 8th centuries. This is the age of the birth of the Welsh nation and the time at which the Welsh language, developed from the ancient Brythonnic language. A number of towns and villages, wells and stones in Wales bear the names of these seintiau, whose interpretation of their faith was often close to nature, and closer to the paganism of the ancient Celts than the politics of the Church of Rome.

One of the early Christians in this ardal, according to legend, was the giant

*1. Maen Twrog; 2. Llandecwyn Church.*

known as Twrog. He became infuriated when he saw pagan rites being performed on the site of the present-day church at Maentwrog, and having observed them from the top of a neighbouring mountain, he picked up a huge rock and hurled it at the congregation below, smashing the altar to smithereens. The stone he hurled, Maen Twrog (*maen*: stone) is to be seen by the corner of the church and has on it an imprint of the giant's thumb and finger.

The early churches along the coast follow the old high-water mark in the days before the embankment was built across Traeth Mawr.

One of these is the church of Llanfihangel-y-traethau one of the churches used by the pilgrims travelling to Bardsey who would worship here before crossing the dangerous trails over Traeth Bach and Traeth Mawr, or before sailing along the coast to Enlli itself. The existing building is comparatively new, but its setting is magical. Such a site is traditional to churches consecrated to Mihangel (St. Michael) in the Celtic lands to this day. Being located betweenearth and sky or land and sea is equivalent to crossing to another world. Because of its link with the sea, a large number of sea captains and mariners from Porthmadog are buried here. An old gravestone in the churchyard from the 12th century and marks the final resting place of 'Wleder, the mother of Hoedliw who built this church during the time of King Owain Gwynedd'.

The old coastline used to reach the parish of Llanfrothen during the Age of the Seintiau and its church, dedicated to another of the Celtic seintiau, Brothen Sant, also has a special ambience. Brothen was the son of Helyg, the lord of a kingdom between Penmaen-mawr and Penmon, a kingdom inundated by the sea in the 5th century according to legend.

*Llanfihangel-y-traethau church*

# Turning back the tide from Traeth Mawr

In summer 2016 nature gave the Porthmadog area a stark reminder that the sea is capable re-claiming land that has been taken from it by human endeavour. During a large and popular festival at nearby Portmeirion, fields near Porthmadog Football Club's ominously named ground, Y Traeth ('the beach') were used as a car park. Heavy rains turned the site into a quagmire and hundreds of motorists were marooned, some of them for days. Global warming and rising sea levels are no longer regarded as merely a topic for academic discussion.

There are iron rings to be seen in the rocks at y Garreg, Llanfrothen. At one time, these would be used to moor ships. The sheer cliffs which today attract so many climbers to the outskirts of Tremadog were once sea cliffs. Two hundred years ago, Traeth Mawr was under the sea and at every high tide, little rocky wooded islets were visible above the waters of the estuary.

In 1798, English-born entrepreneur William Alexander Madocks bought eight farms around Penmorfa and built a tidal embankment to protect the land from the tide in 1800, using the services of an engineer from Lincoln. He recovered some 1,082 acres of land and during the following years utilised them to harvest several crops of corn. Corn prices were high at that time at the height of the Napoleonic Wars and Madocks became a rich man.

In 1801 an act was passed abolishing the Irish parliament and placing that country directly under the aegis of Westminster. This meant there was a need for improved links overland and over the sea between London and Dublin. The A55 from Chester to Holyhead and the A5 from Shrewsbury through Eryri were already receiving attention and being improved. Others favoured the building of a new port for Dublin in Porth Dinllaen, improving the road from Shrewsbury to Dolgellau, across Traeth Mawr to Llŷn. This journey

*1. The Cob at Porthmadog;*
*2. Plas Tan-yr-Allt, Madock's residence;*
*3. The Cob, facing the sea.*

was some 60 kilometres shorter than the route through Chester to Caergybi. But both roads were confronted with natural barriers: Afon Menai on the road to Caergybi, and Traeth Mawr on the road to Porth Dinllaen.

Madocks, now a Member of Parliament, owned land in Penmorfa which was vital to the project. Toll roads were built, the Porth Dinllaen harbour company was established and a pier was constructed there; public houses were built in a bubble of confidence that this would be the trunk road to Dublin. Madocks began constructing a new town, Tremadog, below his home at Tan yr Allt in August 1805.

Tremadog has been carefully designed and although today it is nothing more than a small, quiet town with the unexpected street names of 'Llundain' (London) and 'Dulyn' (Dublin), it has its own particular style which still attracts the attention of students of architecture.

In 1807, an army of 300 labourers began work on constructing an embankment across Traeth Mawr primarily under the supervision of the local agent, John Williams. It cost Madocks £150,000 and took three years to complete the 'cob' which is some 1.5km in length. But after all the hard work, in 1810 parliament decided that Caergybi harbour rather than Porth Dinllaen would be developed as the all important link with Dublin.

This however did not deter the celebrations for the opening of the Cob in September 1811. An ox was roasted and a huge party was held on the Cob itself. There were horse races, a church service, theatrical performances and an eisteddfod.

*1. Tremadog; 2. Dublin Street, Tremadog; 3. Porthmadog harbour.*

# Building a quay in the sand

The centre of the Cob was breached in a dreadful storm in February 1812 and urgent repair work had to be undertaken before the spring tide on 18 March. Throughout the spring of that year, Madocks' debts increased and the English poet Shelley who was staying at Tremadog helped him to raise funds for a while. Following the battle of Waterloo, which brought a long period of warfare to an end and the subsequent return of soldiers to the island of Britain and Ireland. unemployment soared. It was a good opportunity to hire gangs of workers to work on land reclamation schemes.

By a further stroke of good fortune, in changing the course of Afon Glaslyn to flow through sluice gates into the sea, the river's currents created a deep natural pool on the seaward side of the embankment. At the same time, the growth in the slate industry at Blaenau Ffestiniog created a demand for a new port to export their product to the towns which were now springing up following the Industrial Revolution and the development of the New World.

Here was another opportunity for Madocks. The quarries were on the southern side of the river and the pool on the northern side. The trucks from the quarries would have to use the road over the Cob to reach the ships anchored in the pool and Madocks would charge a toll on each and every one of them. He stole a march on the quarry owners and passed the Porthmadog Harbour Act in 1821, which gave Madocks the right to appoint a harbour master and to charge tolls and taxes.

The town and port were not named, as some people assume, after their owner, Madocks, but as a tribute to the 12th century Welsh prince, Madog ab Owain Gwynedd. According to tradition, Madog sailed to the west and discovered America, returning there, with a company of friends, to establish a Welsh colony. One legend maintains that Ynys Fadog, a woody outcrop near the church of Tremadog, was the point from which the adventurer sailed. In 1792, the history came to life again when John Evans, Waunfawr, led a small party along the valley of the Missouri

*Traeth Mawr*

and found white native Americans whose language contained many Welsh words. It was said that these were the descendants of Madog.

Madocks built a new harbour at the end of the Cob and an entire wharf was given to Samuel Holland, from where he would develop the slate export trade over the next 80 years. Madocks died at the age of 55 in Paris before he was able to see Holland's greatest contribution to the development of his port – the construction of a narrow gauge railway in the 1830s. Steam power was replacing the old system of packhorses. In 1831 too, the tax on slates was abolished and there was a huge increase in the prosperity of the new harbour at Porthmadog.

# Slates from Cambrian rocks

Between 1798 and 1825, the price of slates doubled as the demand for housing and factories in the industrial towns increased at a frightening pace.

There had been slate quarries at Ffestiniog since the late 18th century. The industry grew rapidly when Samuel Holland, a slate merchant from Liverpool, opened a quarry on land he had been given by the Oakeley family of Tan y Bwlch and particularly when the son, Samuel Holland, became the manager of the business in 1821. By 1825, Blaenau Ffestiniog was producing 10,000 tonnes of llechi all of which were exported by sea.

Originally, the slates would be brought from the hills on the backs of ponies and loaded onto wagons in Dyffryn Maentwrog. From there they were floated in boats from tiny quays along the banks of Afon Dwyryd to the beaches where ocean-going vessels were waiting.

When the Ffestiniog Railway was built several of the quarries were linked directly to Porthmadog and two major tramways were also built to feed the line –

Cwmorthin (1850) and Rhiw-bach (1863). This region was one of the most efficient in Wales and by the latter half of the 19th century, it was responsible for a third of Welsh slate production. The population of Blaenau and the neighbouring villages of Manod and Tanygrisiau was some 12,000, not counting the army of lodgers who filled every nook and cranny where there was a roof to be had.

Slates were mined underground in the chwareli at Ffestiniog. There are layers of Ordovician slate deep in the rock and broad galleries were opened one under another, with the lowest far below sea level. For every tonne of slate produced, ten tonnes of waste would be extracted from these caverns, and this waste formed tips which rose high above the skyline of the streets of the town.

Throughout the ardal, the remains of old tramlines, quarries and walls built by the quarrymen serve as a memorial to the

*1. Tan y Bwlch; 2. Oakeley Arms, Maentwrog; 3. A slate dresser at Llechwedd; 4. An old quary on the Dwyryd.*

craftsmanship of a bygone age. There are also remains of old inclines used by trucks from some of the highest quarries. The unique innovative spirit of the quarrymen is exemplified in the car gwyllt (wild chariot), a plank of wood on wheels which was used to scoot down the slopes at the end of a hard day's toil in the quarry.

In 1879, the railway tunnel under Bwlch Gorddinan was completed, thereby creating a rail link between Blaenau and Dyffryn Conwy and its estuary. From this time onwards, Chwarel Llechwedd started using this line, the L&NWR, for the export of its slates, loading some of them onto ships at Deganwy quay. There was a huge decline in the slate industry following the two world wars. Quarries were closed, and many people emigrated, and nowadays there are only a handful who work at Gloddfa Ganol, Cwt y Bugail and Llechwedd.

*The slate town of Blaenau Ffestiniog*
*The railway tunnel at Blaenau Ffestiniog*

# The Ffestiniog Railway

Originally, a tramway ran from the chwareli at Ffestiniog southwards along the banks of Afon Dwyryd, descending 200 metres by way of three inclines into the river valley. This line was 0.91 metres in width and linked up the old wharfs with the end of the Cob and the tramway used for building the embankment.

An act of parliament was passed in May 1832 to create a new line linking the quarries of Blaenau Ffestiniog with the new harbour. James Spooner was the surveyor who opened the narrow gauge line in April 1836. For several years, the slate trains from Blaenau used gravity to reach the coast. The empty trucks would then be hauled back up the line by horses, transported in a special wagon on the way down.

The first steam locomotives were seen on the line in 1863 and in 1865. the line began carrying passengers as well as slates. By that time, the quarries at Blaenau were in their heyday, and by the end of the 1860s, over 100,000 tonnes were leaving the area, beating their biggest competitors at Penrhyn and Dinorwig quarries. This was the first time a narrow gauge line carried passengers, but it was a tremendous success and carrying some 250,000 of them during its first year. The service was essential for the industry's survival, for every additional 1,000 tonnes production, the quarry had to employ another 25 quarrymen. With their families, this meant another 100 or so inhabitants. The villages of Blaenau were overflowing with people already, and the terrain prevented any further expansion.

The railway allowed workers who lived as far away as Porthmadog to be within an hour's journey from their workplace. The advantage of the steam train was that the wagons could be filled for the return journey, bringing coal and grain from the harbour in Porthmadog up the line to meet the demand of the town and the quarries. Rather than laying a broader gauge, powerful double locomotives were designed which looked rather like two engines back-to-back, such as the Iarll Meirionnydd (earl of Meirionnydd) which can be seen on the line today.

The slate industry declined during the

*A few of the panoramic views on the Ffestiniog narrow gauge railway*

1. *The end of the line at Blaenau Ffestiniog;*
2. *Tan-y-bwlch station.*

first half of the twentieth century and the line became more dependent on tourism until its closure in 1946. A group was formed to save the line and by 1958 trains were running as far as Tan-y-bwlch. By that time, a reservoir for the production of electricity had been built, drowning the line near Tanygrisiau. A new tunnel was bored, the train reaching Tanygrisiau in 1978 and Blaenau in 1983. Trains still run on a daily basis from the end of March until the beginning of November with the occasional special excursion over Christmas.

# Shipbuilding

For half a century before the building of the Ffestiniog Railway, there was considerable heavy traffic on Afon Dwyryd. The slates were carried on the backs of mules in carts and wagons to the quays at Trwynygarnedd, Cemlyn, Gelligrin and several other pools on the river around Maentwrog and Tan y Bwlch. From there they were loaded into strong locally-built craft designed to travel downriver and out to sea on a regular basis. These boats met up with the larger ships at Ynys Cyngar, often returning with cargos of coal and lime. The boatmen were a rough bunch and they were known locally as *Y Philistiaid* (the Philistines). Each boat could carry up to eight tonnes of slates, and the crew of two would sometimes stand up to their necks in water, in order to load and unload. At one time, there were as many as 40 of these boats on Afon Dwyryd.

Over 50 ships were loaded at Traeth Mawr and Traeth Bach between 1761–1821, before the embankment was built. After the development of Porthmadog harbour, the demand for ships increased and between 1891 and 1913 some of the most elegant and beautiful sailing ships the world has ever seen, according to maritime experts, were built there.

The shipbuilding industry was established in Porthmadog in 1824 when the 65 ton sloop, the Two Brothers was launched at Canol y Clwt, on the site of the present-day Maritime Museum and lifeboat shed. This was the first of 256 ships to be built there, mainly for the slate trade. There were shipbuilding yards at Borth-y-gest and also on the site of the present-day café, garage and car park.

The vessels were known as Western Ocean Yachts, and they were constructed using local oak for the fishing trade in Newfoundland. By that time there was fierce competition between the old sailing ships and the more modern steamships, and the old wooden ships were losing ground to the steamers. But the old seafaring methods were still more profitable in the fishing trade. Porthmadog shipwrights designed wonderful vessels.

*Shipbuilders at Porthmadog, late 19th century*

Portmadoc Harbour.

They were ships of less than 200 tonnes with a crew of some seven or eight. They carried salt from Europe to ports in Canada and salted cod to Genoa and Napoli and other ports in the Mediterranean.

In 1902, 500 ships visited Porthmadog harbour, but the demand for slates declined after the Great War. The town and port saw great changes and pleasure craft and second homes soon filled the gaps left by the old industries. The Maritime Museum recalls past times when the name Porthmadog was familiar to mariners all over the world. The museum is housed in an old single-storey slate shed and as well as displaying pictures of wonderful old ships, there is a collection of different equipment and tools belonging to the old craft.

*1. Porthmadog harbour in the age of the slate vessels; 2. Slate quarry at Bron-y-garth; 3. Sailing ships in the harbour.*

# The shadow of the Western Front

No area in Europe escaped the black clouds of the Great War when it exploded across the continent in 1914. The age of sailing ships came to an end towards that time and the local slate industry began to wane. Technology and engineering developed, and before long the old traditional rural craftsmen in their workshops were unable to compete with the new factories.

The war had a great impact on families and society in general. Many young men went to the trenches never to return, leaving the community scarred and depleted.

The tragedy of war is brought to life when the statistics turn into faces. A single personal story can represent the millions who were lost, and a story of this nature is associated with Trawsfynydd. Even today, the death of the shepherd and bardd (poet) from Cwm Prysor, Hedd Wyn at the battle of Pilkern Ridge in 1917, sums up the utter waste and heartfelt sorrow of the conflict.

Ellis Humphrey Evans (bardic name: Hedd Wyn – ironically Hedd means peace) was born in 1887, the eldest of eleven children. Shortly afterwards, the family moved from a house in Trawsfynydd to his father's home at Yr Ysgwrn – a hill farm a kilometre or so to the east of Trawsfynydd. The family farm still stands to this day, and is farmed by Hedd Wyn's nephew, Gerald.

Ellis began writing poetry at an early age, winning first prize at the age of twelve in a local eisteddfod. He mastered the craft of *cynghanedd* (a strict system of alliteration and assonance) in accordance with the Welsh bardic tradition. He won his first bardic chair at Bala in 1901 and subsequently several other important chairs.

In January 1917, Hedd Wyn was called up into the army. He reached Flanders that summer and by the end of July he and his battalion were in the vicinity of Pilkern Ridge. Hedd Wyn together with many other young men was killed on 31 July.

*1. Hedd Wyn's memorial at Trawsfynydd;*
*2. Y Gadair Ddu ('the black chair').*

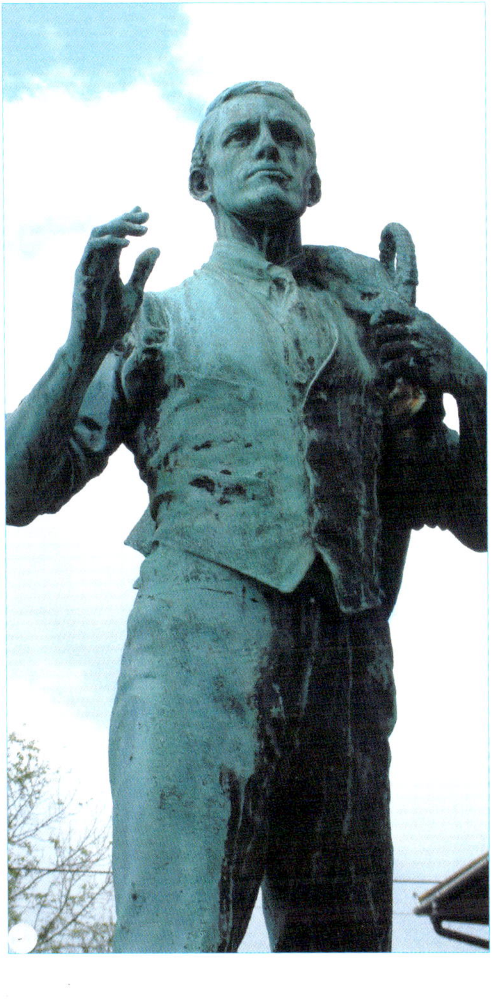

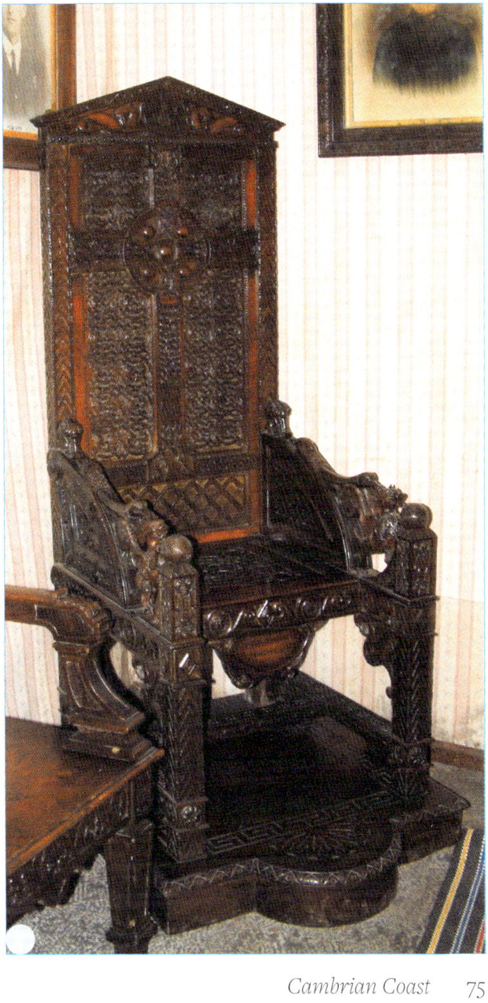

During the months prior to this, he had been working on an awdl (ode) on the subject of *Yr Arwr* (the hero) which he had entered in the competition for the bardic chair at the *Eisteddfod Genedlaethol* ('national eisteddfod') which was being held outside Cymru that year at Birkenhead. He was working on it while in the trenches and he completed it towards the middle of July, On Thursday 6 September, the eisteddfod pavilion was packed. Hedd Wyn's poem was judged to be the winner and the archdruid announced to the crowd that the chaired bard was a soldier who had fallen in France. The audience were in tears and the chair was covered with a black cloak.

The *Gadair Ddu* ('black chair') was carried to Yr Ysgwrn on a special train. The family to this day have kept their word to welcome anyone who calls by to see the chair and to hear the story. A memorial to the poet was unveiled in Trawsfynydd in August 1923 and a heritage centre, Llys Ednowain, was opened in the village in 2004 to present the story and to show the film Hedd Wyn which was nominated for an Oscar in 1991. In 2017, Yr Ysgwrn was restored to its 1917 character and opened its new Heritage Centre to the public, now under the care of the Snowdonia National Park.

1. *Hedd Wyn's grave in Flanders;*
2. *Sunset, at Bryn y Gofeb (hill of Rememberance), Trawsfynydd.*

# The Tranquil Lakes

Beneath the surface of the quiet waters of some of the lakes in this area, there is an invisible power. Not a legendary monster or *tylwyth teg* (fairy folk), but a power to produce electricity.

A dam was built at Trawsfynydd in 1924 and 1928 together with a power station at Maentwrog. A huge lake was formed in the upper reaches of the dyffryn, flooding the wetlands of y Gors Goch together with 24 smallholdings, a chapel and a few cottages. The water was piped to a power station some 200 metres below. The pressure of the water is so enormous that the pipes have to be renewed regularly. In the 1970s, the Tanygrisiau scheme was created with the erection of a dam to deepen Llyn Stwlan on the slopes of Moelwyn Mawr. The water is released to the power station at Tanygrisiau some 300 metres below and is stored in a specially built pool there. Then, during the night, electricity is used from the national grid to pump the water back up the mountain to supply the next day's demand.

By way of compensation for clearing Llyn Stwlan of its fish stocks, the electricity board donated five thousand trout to Cymdeithas Enweiriol Cambrian, the local angling society, to be released in Llynnoedd Gamallt on Y Migneint. There is also fishing in the bounteous lower lake at Tanygrisiau. There is a long tradition of fishing lakes in the ardal and a number of fishing flies have been designed over the years which are still favourites with local fishermen. Cymdeithas y Cambrian was established in 1885 and in the same year, a local quarry owner presented 15,000 Loch Leven trout as a gift to Llynnoedd Gamallt. The Society ensured fishing rights on a number of other mountain lakes around Ffestiniog and Trawsfynydd. Nurseries were created to breed local trout and boat-houses were built on the shores of some of the lakes. These days international angling competitions are held at Llyn Trawsfynydd.

In the early 1960s, Llyn Trawsfynydd was drained and work was commenced to prepare for the first inland nuclear power station in Britain. The lake was extended and the dam reinforced. The lake's waters

*Llyn Tanygrisiau*

were to be warmed by radioactive rods to produce steam to spin the turbines. Walls were built in the lake itself to ensure the water circulated well, and the atomic power station began generating electricity in 1965. Production stopped way back in 1991 but the complex decommissioning process goes on. Meanwhile the power station at Maentwrog continues to produce electricity unabated. There is now

a visitor centre on the site of the old atomic plant and there are pleasure trips on the lake itself.

In early September, an annual fishing and walking festival is held in the Ffestiniog area, including guided walks by local naturalists and historians. It is worth walking to the lakes to enjoy their beauty and to fish from their shores.

*1. Cwm Ystradllyn and Gorseddau quarry;*
*2. Llyn Trawsfynydd, dawn*

# Chwarel Llechwedd today

Planning regulations now stipulate that Welsh slates must be used to roof some of the buildings of Cymru. This has provided a spark of new life into the old industry.

Today, there is a new respect for the craft of the quarrymen and roofer. In the church of Dewi Sant in Blaenau Ffestiniog, the stained-glass windows are a tribute to the old craftsmen, and the use of slates in walls and buildings are a means of clearing old spoil heaps. Recently, slates from Blaenau were used in the construction of Canolfan y Mileniwm (The Millennium Centre) in Caerdydd (Cardiff).

However, there is no doubt that the most fitting tribute to life in the quarries is to be found in a dedicated centre at Chwarel Llechwedd. In 1980, it was awarded the first prize throughout Britain as the best visitor attraction. The public are transported down the incline to the depths of the caverns in modern carriages and are given a taste of the working conditions of the quarrymen. The quarry has been running tourist trains along one of the old tramways since 1972, and within five years a million visitors had made the journey. Llechwedd leads the field in terms of industrial heritage tourism and is one of Europe's most renowned interpretative centres.

The area began trading in slates for the first time in 1799, when Chwarel Diffwys was opened, which is now part of Llechwedd. At the time a total of 732 people were living in Blaenau. The industry was not particularly prosperous until 1849 when a gang of men, who at that time were working without pay, blasted a tunnel some 18 metres into the rock under what is now the mouth of one the tunnels for the tourist train. A rich underground vein of grey-blue slate was discovered which would revolutionise the future of the quarry and the town.

The mining work has created sixteen levels in Llechwedd, each one identified by a letter. There is a chain of adits and pillars on each level, with the pillars carefully

*1. Above Llechwedd and Oakeley quarries;*
*2. Llechwedd slate workshops today*
*3. Going underground at Llechwedd.*

placed one above the other in line to a depth of some 300 metres below the surface. The rockmen would work on the rock face freeing great blocks of slate. These would be transported in trucks to be dressed in the workshops on the surface and the waste would be taken to the spoil heaps by the apprentice quarrymen.

1. *Celebrating Ffestiniog slate heritage;*
2. *The recreated slate village at Llechwedd;*
3. *Visiting Llechwedd;*
4. *General view of Blaenau Ffestiniog.*

This is all brought to life in a visit to Llechwedd where you can appreciate the grain and character of the rock as well as the remarkable craft of those who work it. In a competition in 1872, the crowd was amazed by a quarryman from Llechwedd who was able to split a block 5cms thick into 45 slates. Today, the craftsmen who make fans and other decorative artefacts from slate are managing to split 35 layers to every 2.5cm. As well as exploring the deep quarries there is plenty of opportunity in Llechwedd to be amazed by, and to purchase the fine products made by today's craftsmen.

# Highland Railway and the Maritme Museum

A new narrow gauge railway was driven through the heart of Snowdonia in 1922 when the Welsh Highland Company combined with a number of lines which were already in existence between Caernarfon and Porthmadog. One section was a horse-drawn tramway which carried slates down from the quarries of Cwm Croesor to Porthmadog. The tram rails were modified to take steam locomotives and a new track was laid linking Croesor junction with the line to Rhyd-ddu. During the 1930s the Ffestiniog Railway was given a lease on the Welsh Highland Railway, but the line was not a success and was closed in 1937.

In 1961, a society was formed to reopen that line. By 1980, trains were running along a short stretch of track from Porthmadog to Pen-y-mownt and the company still operates this service. They also opened a museum in one of the old engine sheds near the station at Porthmadog. On display are a collection of engines, wagons and carriages from different periods together with relics and artefacts from the time when the railway was in operation. There are a number of remarkable photographs on display and the museum provides an insight into the hustle and bustle of the old days.

In 1995, the Ffestiniog Railway managed to acquire the assets of the old Welsh Highland Railway Company with the intention of opening the line all the way from Caernarfon to Porthmadog, a magnificent journey of 40 kilometres, With the help of the lottery fund, the line was opened from Caernarfon to Dinas in 1997. By 2002, the train had reached Waunfawr and in 2004, Rhyd-ddu station was reopened. The intention is to bring the line as far as Porthmadog by 2009.

The area of Y Cei in Porthmadog is full of the heritage of the old days, when ships from the town sailed the oceans of the world. At the end of the Cob are the sluice-gates and Llyn Bach (the inner harbour – 'little lake') which controls the flow of Afon Glaslyn to the sea in accordance with

*The Welsh Highland Railway*

*The Welsh Highland Railway at Aberglaslyn crossing Pont Croesor*

*The Welsh Highland Railway above Beddgelert*

the tide. Near the bridge is the site of the wharves used by Greaves and Holland to load llechi onto the ships. There is another large wharf closer to the estuary than Pencei. Today it is the site of boat workshops. Opposite this quay lies Ynys y Balast. When ships returned empty or with light cargoes, they would have to take on a cargo of rocks from a foreign port which would be placed at the bottom of the ship to stabilise her at sea. Ships would jettison this ballast at the mouth of the Porthmadog harbour, and seeds among the rocks would germinate. Consequently the site has now become an island of exotic plant species! A little further downstream is Borth-y-gest which, at one time, was the site of important shipyards and the houses of the local pilots.

Behind Y Ganolfan – the community centre – in Porthmadog, is an interesting maritime museum depicting the romance and harshness of life at sea, displaying relics and various bits of tackle from the old ships.

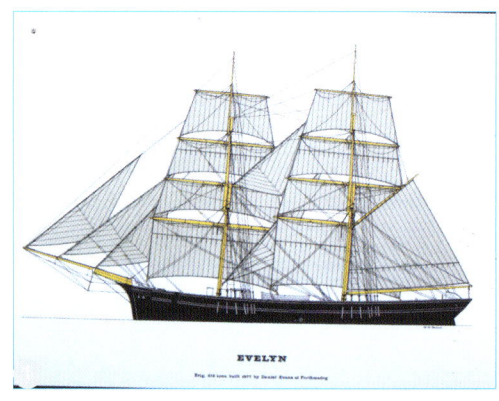

EVELYN

*1. A drawing of a Porthmadog schooner;*
*2. In the Martime Museum;*
*3. Porthmadog Harbour.*

# Y Plas and the National Park

Plas Tan y Bwlch stands at the heart of the Eryri National Park in a magnificent location overlooking the wooded slopes and green river valley of Afon Dwyryd. The Park was formed in 1949 and was one of the earliest national parks in Britain. Plas Tan-y-bwlch is now a centre for environmental studies, offering courses on the countryside and the natural and cultural heritage of this part of Cymru.

When the Park boundaries were drawn up, it was decided not to include Blaenau Ffestiniog with its tomenni llechi, its terraced housing and other industrial scars. Ironically, it was the wealth from these chwareli which built this beautiful plas, which is now a study centre, at Tan y Bwlch. This was the family home of the Oakeleys, slate owners as well as landlords over vast tracts of local land. Today, an equal value is placed on industrial heritage and the Plas now provides courses on this aspect of the local treftadaeth as well.

The woods around the Plas itself contain numerous delightful paths which can be walked as well as an opportunity to admire the gardens with its crafted steps. The 100-acre estate is dotted with rare species of trees and shrubs stretching down to the shores of the magical lake of Llyn Mair. In the Plas itself, the wood and stonework is indicative of the riches which were hewn from the great slate caverns. In the midst of all the grandeur of yesteryear, there is high quality provision for conferences and accommodation, all in keeping with the 21st century.

Although the beauty of the gardens at the Plas blend very agreeably with the natural beauty of Eryri, there is also respect shown for the contrast they provide. Originally many visitors tended to consider the term 'national parks' to mean leisure parks, while another group of conservationists wanted to get rid of any agricultural activity and to turn them into a natural wilderness.

The beauty of Eryri would not be as it is today were it not for the community which has lived on the shores, river valleys and slopes for thousands of years. The crafts and the natural conservation which

*Plas Tan y Bwlch*

have been part and parcel of the farming communities have shaped and created the character of this part of the world. The Park now recognises that the intrinsic beauty of Eryri cannot continue without the support and the continued existence of the local community and natural conservation is seen to go hand in hand with the protection of the rights of a Welsh-speaking community and its inherent culture.

*Overleaf: 1. The Plas above Dwyryd river; 2. The gardens at Plas Tan y Bwlch.*

# Craftsmen today and yesterday

Craftsmen and agricultural workshops were very prevalent in the ardal at one time. The work of the stonemasons of the past is very much in evidence in the dry stone walls in the fields and on the high slopes of the mountains. This craft is still very much alive. On the other hand, the wool factory in Cwm Croesor has long since closed its doors together with the leather works at Tremadog and Llanfrothen and the corn mills and lime kilns scattered throughout the area. Tremadog was the site of the first woollen factory in Cymru to use steam-powered machinery.

A particularly attractive gallery is that of the local artist, Rob Piercy in Stryd yr Wyddfa, Porthmadog backing on to a colourful courtyard full of flowers. This has been the location the gallery since 1980 and Rob Piercy is now a highly acclaimed artist throughout Wales. The mountains are a constant inspiration to him, particularly the views which are to be seen from the higher mountain routes – as one might expect of someone who is himself fond of mountaineering. His work has an honesty which stems from Rob's all-weather, all-season approach. As well as original paintings and prints by Rob Piercy himself, there are often exhibitions of pictures and artwork by other local artists at the gallery (www.robpiercy.com).

There are several craftshops in the busy Stryd Fawr of Porthmadog, including the famous Portmeirion Pottery shop.

*Rob Piercy's studio and gallery at Porthmadog*

# Portmeirion

Unfortunately, the tourist industry is often responsible for a myriad of dreadful buildings and tasteless developments which today scar the land and shores of Wales. By way of contrast, tourism is also responsible for the existence of Portmeirion.

The concept of Portmeirion emanated from the conversion of a house at Aber-iâ, the peninsula lying between the estuaries of Glaslyn and Dwyryd, into a hotel in 1926. A little prior to this, the owners, the architect Clough Williams-Ellis and his wife Annabel of Plas Brondanw in Llanfrothen, were wondering what to do with this wild, wooded peninsula and came very close to selling it. Then, Clough Williams-Ellis' imagination was fired as he saw an opportunity to express both his craft and what was closest to his heart.

Between the two world wars, Clough had spent a great deal of time sailing, and on one of his trips, he came across the village of Portfino in Italy. This experience influenced his dream at that time to find an island where he could build his own creation. Then it suddenly dawned on him that in fact there was nowhere better than the wild peninsula of Aber-iâ, less than 8 kms from his home.

From the outset, Portmeirion had to create an income which could be reinvested in the dream. It was an economic venture with an emphasis on leisure. According to Clough himself, there was something of the spirit of a noson lawen (traditional evening of entertainment) with regard to the work that took place but great care was given to the detail of every building, statue, path, stream and shrub. It provides a heart-warming protest against the excesses of contemporary architecture and is a visual showpiece.

Today 100,000 visitors a year come to see the village, to spend a day, drifting round the grounds and loitering in the charming little shops, or to stay for a few days in order to absorb Portmeirion's continental atmosphere, to feast in the hotel or to celebrate weddings and social gatherings in Hercules' hall. In every season and in every weather, the village

*Portmeirion from across the estuary*

has its own special magic and romance, the swift ebb and flow of the estuary reflecting the comings and goings of the village itself.

Castell Deudraeth, which stands between Portmeirion and Minffordd has recently been restored and the hotel and restaurant are now an additional resource. The original castle on the site was built by Gruffydd ap Cynan around 1175, making it one of the earliest Welsh castles to be built in stone. That castle is mentioned by Geraldus de Cambrensis in his "Journeys through Wales".

Little of that earlier castle remained in the mid 19th century when the property was aquired by David Williams. Williams, a wealthy attorney, built a fanciful villa in mock-Gothic style on a high promontory overlooking Portmeirion village.

Clough's grandson, Robin Llywelyn, is the chief executive of the trust which was formed to protect the heritage, and while the architecture may be Italian, the croeso at Portmeirion is entirely Welsh.

*1. Portmeirion in all its colours; 2. The hotel;*
*3. The estuary from Portmeirion;*
*4. Castell Deudraeth.*

# Storms and blue sky

The ebb and flow in the aberoedd of the Dwyryd and Mawddach rivers in Meirionnydd brings a change to the scenery with every passing hour. Over the centuries, raging storms have shifted the sandbanks along the entire length of this coastline. The sea, and those whose livelihoods has followed its course, have had a profound influence on the character of Ardudwy – the old name for the *cantref* (hundred) which includes both Harlech and Barmouth.

Some of the early legends of the Mabinogi and Cantre'r Gwaelod are integral to Ardudwy's history. They describe how the land was swallowed by the waves and how a fleet of ships from Ireland were welcomed by the king Brân at Harlech.

As well as the wealth of history and culture, nature in all its glory is also to be seen at its very best in Ardudwy. From its blue-green lakes in the high *cymoedd* (pl. of *cwm* – mountain valley) to panoramic sunsets over the western waves – the tremendous variety on display throughout every season of the year is hard to beat.

*Ynys Fochras ('shell island') on the coast with the Rhinogydd in the background*

# Ancient stones

Stones are an essential element of Ardudwy and parts of the landscape are reminiscent of Conamara and western Ireland. The fields are separated by sturdy high stone walls, the result of hard labour at the time of the land enclosures some two or three centuries ago.

In Bwlch Tyddiad the so-called 'Roman Steps' follow a prehistoric path climbing from Cwm Bychan in Ardudwy through a gap in the Rhinogydd towards the east. At some point – possibly during the era of the packhorse in the Middle Ages – stone steps were placed along the path, to make it easier for horses to cross from Harlech to the Trawsfynydd valley. There are very few Roman remains in Ardudwy – overland routes were fundamental to their empire and the Romans would have considered the locality to the west of the Rhinogydd as being inaccessible.

The Bwlch Tyddiad steps are only one of a number of ancient tracks which lead from the coast through the hills – evidence of how succesive waves of migrants and visitors have made landfall on this coast from the New Stone Age onwards.

There are six cromlechi (dolmens) dating back to about 2500 BC within a five mile radius of Harlech. These are *cromlechi porth* (portal dolmens) and the two most notable examples are can be seen behind the school in Dyffryn Ardudwy. The two now stand separately but the remains of the large *tomen* (earth mound) nearby suggest that they were originally part of a single memorial. The cromlechi consist of two huge stones facing each other, forming a gateway surmounted by a slanting capstone. As is usual with such designs, the gateway was closed symbolically with a slightly smaller stone.

The capstones are smooth and flat underneath and rough and convex on the upper side, suggesting that the underside was visible to those entering the burial chamber but that the upper surface was covered by a mound of stones and earth.

*Bwlch Tyddiad's ancient track*

1. *Bryn Cader Faner – Bronze Age cairn;*
2. *Inscribed standing stone at Llanfihangel-y-traethau; 3. Carneddi Hengwm.*

# The church in the sands

There was a theory doing the rounds that the name Llandanwg is a shortened version of Llan-dan-wg-y-môr – the church beneath the wrath of the sea. That would be a fair description of a church built near Llanbedr among sand dunes, only a few feet above sea level, but the truth iss is more conventional. Like many churches on this coastline it is dedicated to a Celtic saint, in this case Tanwg who arrivd from Llydaw with Cadfan, founder of the monastic sefflement on Ynys Enlli.

In a vicious storm in the nineteenth century, the sea smashed the wall of Llandanwg cemetery and the gravestones were buried under great mounds of sand. Most of the gravestones were saved and the church was cleared of sand after that, but it stands today enclosed by the sand-dunes. One of the graves under the eastern window of the church is inscribed with the letters 'I.Ph'. This is believed to be the grave of Siôn Phylip of Mochras, a renowned 16th century poet from Ardudwy.

We cannot leave Llandanwg without mentioning the church bell, which has a less saintly Celtic connection than the church's Breton founder. The bell's former home was at a small mansion called Doonbeg House in County Sligo in Ireland. When the Irish Free State was set up in 1922 after the War of Independence, tenants of Doobeg House rebelled against their landlord, Charles Phibbs. Phibbs was a member of a wealthy English Protestant family whose father, also called Charles, had had a longstanding conflict his tenants over rents and other issues. After his death in 1916 his son inherited the estate and was seen as being the main supporter of the British in the area during the War of Independence.

Things got worse when the war ended and the family lost its protection from the British. There were arson attacks and shots fired. Then in May 1922 a grave was dug in front of the house bearing the crude epitaph:

*Llandanwg Church in the sands*

Here lies the remains of Charles Phibbs who died with a ball of lead in his ribs.

Phibbs took the sensible course of departing immediately, but not before a family member had taken a photograpf of him standing in his own 'grave'. Possibly because of family commections, he ended up in Ardudwy and bought a 100-acre farm called Plas Gwynfryn. The following year he made a discreet visit to Doonbeg House to retrieve some possession he'd been forced to leave behind in his haste. Among them was the bell that had been uses to summon the servants from the fields at mealtimes, which he gave as a gift to the church at nearby Llandanwg where it can still be seen in the bell tower.

*Llyn Cwm Bychan above Harlech*

# A Norman Castle

After centuries of sustained resistance, the military capability of the Welsh eventually succumbed to one of the most costly invasions of the Middle Ages in 1282–3. Edward I – the king of England at the time – was one of the greediest and most merciless monarchs of his age and through a combination of a strong naval force, mercenaries from every corner of Europe and a bottomless fund of money, he succeeded in conquering the north-west, and in overwintering there. When Llywelyn II, the leader of the Welsh, was killed in an ambush at Cilmeri in 1282, the Welsh lost their prince and the will to fight to safeguard their identity.

It was a superficial victory for the foreign army however. It soon became obvious to Edward that he would have to prepare for the next rebellion by the Welsh. This was achieved by building a chain of huge castles around the heartland of Snowdonia. This was the costliest scheme of its kind in Europe during the Middle Ages – a manifestation of the danger which Edward still perceived as being posed by the Welsh.

Harlech was the southernmost of those castles. There had originally been a Welsh castle there but any remains thereof were destroyed by the king of England's designer, James St George of Savoy in France. St George had already won acclaim as a military architect and he followed Edward to Wales to supervise the work of erecting strong, new fortifications at Conwy, Caernarfon, Harlech and Beaumaris. They were built for warfare, and are situated close to the sea to facilitate their supply in times of crisis, and are strategically located in a powerful position from which to challenge the hinterland.

All the Edwardian castles have a unique character and Harlech is no exception: from the outside it has a striking and powerful appearance, standing shoulder to shoulder with the peaks of Snowdonia, but inside it is more homely and compact. It has the same atmosphere as a large mansion, with

*Harlech castle against the splendor of Snowdonia. Overleaf: 1. Harlech castle - Glyndŵr's principal seat during the Welsh revolt of 1400–15; 2. A western light on Harlech castle.*

rather a neat courtyard and fine windows in its inner walls – a castle which could also serve as a family residence.

Harlech castle was completed in 1290, in good time to withstand the great Welsh uprising of 1294–5 under the leadership of Madog ap Llywelyn. At that time, the sea and maritime support was key to the garrison's ability to hold their ground in the face of incursions by the Welsh.

In contrast to the other castles, Edward did not establish a borough in the shadow of Harlech castle to attract merchants and foreign government officials to colonise the country. No privileged town was created here to oppress the Welsh, but that did not prevent Welsh forces from attacking the castle once again during another rebellion in 1400.

*Inside Harlech castle*

# The home and senedd of Owain Glyndŵr

It is ironic that the most famous person ever to make his home in Harlech castle was the Welsh national hero Owain Glyndŵr. It was obvious that he too had an eye for a favourable site.

Wales had suffered more than a century of barbaric government in the shadow of Edward I's castles and towns. A huge number of men and boys had been killed as a precaution in case of rebellion and according to English records, hundreds more women, children and old people were also slaughtered. After 1282, taxes in Wales increased by six hundred per cent – the English crown was bankrupt after the costly war. Then, the first anti-Welsh laws were passed – the Welsh could neither hold office nor possess land in a town nor trade beyond the walls of a town; they were not allowed to carry arms and unable to accuse an Englishman of committing any offence; Cymraeg (the Welsh language) was forbidden as a public language and a Welshman could be executed without the sanction of a court of law if he were caught in a town after nightfall.

Six hundred years ago, the Welsh had had enough of this racial oppression. Owain of Glyndyfrdwy, which lies to the south of Rhuthun, rose up as a leader and together with three hundred followers, attacked the town of Rhuthun and razed it to the ground in September 1400. Over the years that followed every English town in Wales was attacked and burnt; many of the 'castles of conquest' were attacked too, several even being successfully captured.

One of the castles which fell into the hands of Glyndŵr's army in the spring of 1404 was Harlech. He moved his headquarters and family there, and for four years this had a very positive effect on his campaign. During that period Glyndŵr received a number of European ambassadors there and in 1405 and 1406, a Welsh *senedd* (parliament) was held there three times.

A large English army of some one thousand men, arrived to besiege Harlech castle in 1408. It was a long siege

*Harlech Castle*

# Owain Glyndŵr a Harlech

# the Owain Glyndwr holding of Harlech

Erbyn 1402 'ai Owain o nerth i nerth: ddwy flynedd yn ddiweddarach, gallai i bob pwrpas hawlio mai ef a lywodraethai Cymru gyfan.

By 1402 Owain Glyndwr was going from success to success: two years later he could claim to be effective ruler of virtually all of Wales.

**1404**

**the climax 1405**

**decline 1406-07**

**1408-09**

Ym Mai 1404, cipiodd Glyndŵr ei wobr fawr – castell Aberystwyth a Harlech; nid rhyddhaeyn ei ... ni nes i ... iawn, bydd ... hyn ... rai ... yn llaw rryn ... eu ... ddeulu ... ... gado lys. Y ... h ... ... ... swn ... yn ...

In May 140...

The name of Owain Glyndwr is perhaps most conjured with in all of Welsh history –

synonymous in Wales with the assertion national identity and immortalised in even by Shakespeare. And yet he rem shadowy and elusive figure.

Born between 1349 and 1359 of an ancestry that allowed him, later, to lineal succession from the princes Powys and of South Wales, he wa also related to the English royal of Tudor. For some years he stu at the Inns of Court in Westmin then turned instead ...

throughout the spring and summer and was met by staunch Welsh resistance. Traces of the prolonged bombardment are still to be seen on the defences, which resulted in the castle's evacuation in February 1409. Marged, Owain's wife and Catrin, his daughter and her children were taken to the Tower of London but Owain himself managed to escape.

After the promise of Glyndŵr's ascendancy, when the foundations of modern Wales were laid in both word and deed, Glyndŵr's fortunes started to ebb. He was under constant pressure from the English armies and the country became gravely impoverished as a result of the continuing state of war. After fifteen years of rebellion, Owain and his small band of faithful followers disappeared from the history books to the world of mythology. It is not known where he died, but his great dream of Wales enjoying full national status amongst the countries of Europe, lives on.

*1. & 3. Parts of the Glyndŵr exhibition at the castle; 2. A harness piece found at Harlech, with Glyndŵr's arms on it.*

# The Manorhouses of Ardudwy

As Glyndŵr's story became legend, the responsibility for defending different areas of Wales from the oppressive English penal laws fell to the noblemen. Various families from the great mansions of Ardudwy – Maes-y-neuadd, Cwm Bychan, Corsygedol and others, were descendants of the old Welsh princes. They maintained the traditional role of the Welsh nobleman – defending their land and people and providing patronage for the poets and local culture.

In the 15th century, the Welsh were looking for a national leader to succeed Glyndŵr. People started to whisper the name of Harri, one of the descendants of the Tudur family from Penmynydd, Môn, who was in exile in Llydaw, but through his grandfather's marriage could claim succession to the English throne through the House of Lancaster.

The Welsh uchelwyr gave their support to the victorious Harri Tudur, but having attained the throne in London, the king disregarded the needs of his fellow Welsh to a large extent. Some of the noblemen became quite Anglicised in their language and ways, going to live in London and forgetting about their people back home. Others stayed true to the dreams of the Welsh.

One of these was General Henry Lloyd, Cwm Bychan, one of the Llwyd family, who was descended from the Princes of Powys. He saw an opportunity to strike a blow against the English crown in his support for the Jacobeans. He went to France, became involved with the Irish Brigade who supported any enemy of England and joined the Jacobean rebellion in 1745.

Ellis Wynne was one of the Wynn family from Maes-y-neuadd on his mother's side. He inherited the plasty of Lasynys near Harlech and became the rector of Llandanwg parish in 1704. He was the author of a work of colourful prose which satirises sinners on their way to hell, and is one of the great classics of Welsh literature. Maes-y-neuadd was for many

*Maes-y-neuadd*

YN Y TY HWN
Y GANED·Y BU FYW·Y BU FARW·
**ELLIS WYNNE**
1671–1734
AWDUR GWELEDIGAETHEU
Y BARDD CWSC
"A DDARLLENNO YSTYRIED
A YSTYRIO COFIED"
ER COF AMDANO·AC ER PARCH
I'W ENW·Y GOSODWYD YMA'R
GARREG HON·AWST MCMXXII

years a luxurious hotel and restaurant but ran into financial difficulty and is closed at the time of writing. Lasynys belongs to a local trust, who have restored it to its former glory and opened its doors to the public.

*The restored manor of Lasynys*

# The Drovers' Roads

From the end of the Middle Ages until the arrival of the railways, the Welsh drovers would drive thousands of cattle, sheep, pigs and geese each year from the mountain pastures to the rich grasslands of south-east England to be fattened up for the markets there. This was a journey of hundreds of miles, often over rough, and remote highland terrain. Amongst the dangers were wolves, highwaymen as well as severe weather conditions. Wales had its Wild West and its heroes on the droving trails long before Hollywood romanticised the cowboys of the New World.

The slopes, mountains and river valleys of Ardudwy and also the western peninsula of Llŷn were ideal for rearing good stock. The porthmyn would be local men, since the farmers were entrusting them with responsibility for their livestock throughout the journey. Each droving expedition contained an element of financial risk and investment. Blacksmiths were paid to shoe the cattle and sheep and for putting leather shoes or tar and sand on the feet of the geese before driving them over the mountains. At their journey's end, the porthmyn would be at the mercy of the marketplace and were responsible for ensuring the safe delivery of money back to Ardudwy which would be needed to support the local economy for another year. It is hardly surprising that the porthmyn were referred to as the 'Welsh Armada'. Although there are stories about an occasional deceitful porthmon (sing. of porthmyn) absconding with the takings from the market, generally speaking porthmyn were highly respected individuals.

Drovers crossed Traeth Mawr from Llŷn and tackled the Rhinogydd passes behind Harlech with Ardudwy droves, before going on over the Meirionnydd uplands eastwards of Trawsfynydd.

*The 'Drover's tree' on a mountain road to the east of Trawsfynydd*

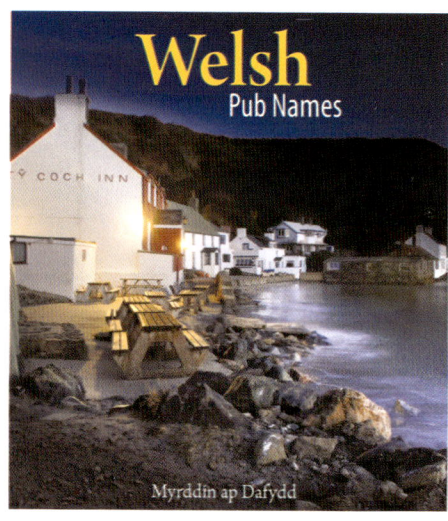

Welsh **Pub Names**

Myrddin ap Dafydd

Welsh —— Place Names ——

Llŷn
the peninsula and its past EXPLORED